EKLAVYA'S
SKYWARD JOURNEY

ADITYA NARAYAN

INDIA • SINGAPORE • MALAYSIA

Copyright © Aditya Narayan 2024
All Rights Reserved.

This book has been published with all efforts taken to make the material error-free after the consent of the author. However, the author and the publisher do not assume and hereby disclaim any liability to any party for any loss, damage, or disruption caused by errors or omissions, whether such errors or omissions result from negligence, accident, or any other cause.

While every effort has been made to avoid any mistake or omission, this publication is being sold on the condition and understanding that neither the author nor the publishers or printers would be liable in any manner to any person by reason of any mistake or omission in this publication or for any action taken or omitted to be taken or advice rendered or accepted on the basis of this work. For any defect in printing or binding the publishers will be liable only to replace the defective copy by another copy of this work then available.

Eklavya's Skyward Journey is a work of fiction. The names, incidents and characters portrayed in it are the product of the manifestations of the author's imagination and their personal experiences and opinions. Any resemblances with actual persons, living or dead are entirely coincidently.

All rights reserved in all media. No part of this publication can be reproduced, stored in a retrieval system or transmitted in any form, without the written permission of the authors.

It is the author's responsibility to ensure that his or her work is free and clear of any counts of libel, plagiarism, breach of privacy or misinterpretation of facts. The publishers are not responsible for it.

Additionally, the images including the cover page, back cover and images associated with each poem were generated with OpenAI's Dall E software. Subject to the Content Policy and Terms, users own the images they create with DALL•E, including the right to reprint, sell, and merchandise – regardless of whether an image was generated through a free or paid credit.

Eklavya lived in a crowded slum in Mumbai, India, where his father worked as a driver and his mother was a servant in a neighbouring apartment. But Eklavya's dreams were big and bright!

He went to a government school that didn't have many books or computers.

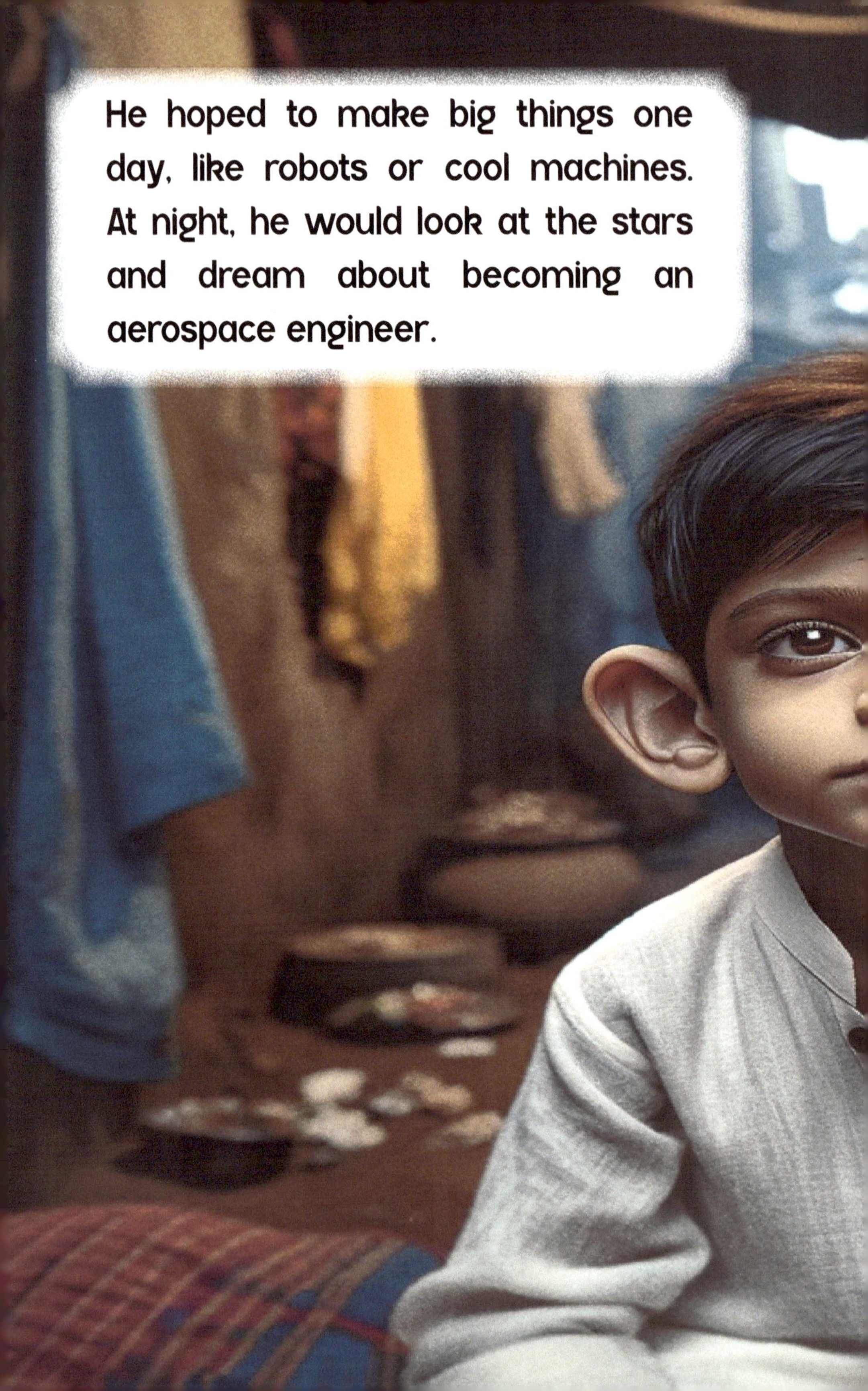
He hoped to make big things one day, like robots or cool machines. At night, he would look at the stars and dream about becoming an aerospace engineer.

Eklavya loved to learn, especially about how things worked and why.

Even as a little boy, Eklavya loved gadgets and would often fix old radios and toys.

A few years later, school was still hard for Eklavya. He didn't get good marks and some kids made fun of him.

But he didn't give up. He loved learning how things worked and kept trying. He also learned to fix old laptops that people threw away.

Eklavya wanted to be good at both his hobby and studies. Sometimes, it was hard to focus on school when he loved working with his hands so much.

One day, some new mentors came to Eklavya's school with boxes full of science experiments and technological parts. They taught in a fun way, called 'Hands-On Learning' with lots of experiments and projects to do.

Eklavya was excited to see experiments and models that he could touch and build. This new way of learning helped Eklavya understand better and his school grades started to get better.

He built his first drone from parts the mentors brought and loved seeing it fly.

Soon, he convinced the full community to join in. The kids who used to make fun of him now thought his drone was really interesting.

Eklavya's parents saw how happy and smart he was becoming, as he used technology. It was hard to keep up with school and his tech projects, but Eklavya tried his best.

He spends his evenings under a flickering streetlight, books spread out, diving into mathematics and science after rushing back from school.

Over time, he became really good with technology and his school marks went up too.

Years went by, and Eklavya finished school with good grades. He got a scholarship to go to college because of his hard work.

He still had his dream of being an aerospace engineer, and knew he had to work hard to get there.

In college, Eklavya studied hard and learned all about space and rockets. He graduated top of his class, but that wasn't enough for him.

After college, Eklavya became an aerospace engineer, just like he had always dreamed. He worked on planes that fly around the world, big rockets that went to space and even helped design a satellite.

Eklavya never forgot where he came from and often visited his old school, inspiring the students there with his gadgets.

Eklavya realized that this divide in society between people who are from underprivileged background and those who have access to resources, could be solved by increasing access to technology.

So, he also started a small program to teach technology to kids in his slum.

Eklavya's story shows that no matter where you start, you can reach the stars if you work hard and never give up.

This book was dedicated to my 'first ever' batch of robotics students with Project Yantrikta,

Hilal, Sarfaraj, Shivani, Ranganath, Richard, Razia, Rumana, Vikash, Gurukiran, Khushi, Ronija, Anuj, Suman, Elisha, Abdul, Baban, Niraj, Sakirul, Ishika, Toufik, Manoj, Anjali, Pallavi, Bikash, Bhaskar, Muskan, Dilbas, Deep, Sandeep, Bishwajit, Zubair, Tasleem, Nargis, Anamika, Nibin, Saniya, Priyadarshani, Arisha Sahil, Pratima, Chandrika, Shiva, Veerabhadra, Priya, Nazeem, Suvarna, Ramesh, Basavaraj, Shambhavi, Gagan, Chikkaswamy, Baralinga, Sahana, Manil Chandra, Ramu, Rajesh, Shashi, Tanushree, Aruthi and Praveen.

At Ramagondanahalli Government School, Siddapura Government School, Immedihalli Government School, Basavanagar Government School, Seegehalli Government School among others.

Awards Ceremony at Immedihalli Government School

About the Author

Aditya Narayan is a rising junior at Inventure Academy in Bangalore, India. He has submitted poems for previous anthologies by the Impish Lass Publishing House, and recently published his own anthology, titled: "Silhouettes of Time."

Intrinsically motivated and passionate, he actively seeks out innovation and enjoys routinely challenging himself. Aditya is interested in the application of mathematical concepts in present-day computer science and artificial intelligence. Aditya became cognizant of the importance of science and technology among the youth in developing countries. This led to him founding Project Yantrikta (projectyantrikta.org), a robotics program for underprivileged students across Bangalore. He recently spoke about his project and the lack of STEM exposure at the 1M1B Activate summit in the United Nations, in November 2023.

Apart from his immense love for writing, Aditya was elected as the school captain on the student council, with leadership being a trait that has always come naturally to him. An avid public speaker and debater, he has served as the head-delegate of his school's Model UN delegation. This foray into public speaking does not end here however, he is also a drama enthusiast, performing in multiple Broadway-style production musicals over the years.

Further details about the author can be found at linkedin.com/in/adityanarayan8/